The Book of Us

The Story of

_____ & _____
(name)   (name)

_____
(The date we met)

The Book of Us

A Journal of Your Love Story
in 150 Questions

Kate & David Marshall

HYPERION
New York

Designed by KimShala Wilson

Library of Congress Cataloging-in-Publication Data

Marshall, Kate
    The book of us : a journal of your love story in 150 questions / by Kate & David Marshall.
        p.   cm.
    1. Marriage—Miscellanea.   2. Spouses—Miscellanea.   3. Love—Miscellanea.   4. Diaries.   I. Marshall, David.
    II. Title.
HQ734.M184742   1998
306.872—dc21   98–37754
                                                                              CIP
    ISBN 0-7868-6477-X

FIRST EDITION
10 9 7 6

To Our Parents

SALLY, TOM, RUTH AND GENE

You showed us how to love.

Contents

How to Write Your Love Story

How?

- This journal gives you 150 prompts to help you tell your own love story. You answer the prompts with as much or as little detail as you want.

- The five main sections of the journal cover the complete life span of your relationship, from your first date to your golden anniversary and everything in between. It is up to you to decide where one section leaves off and the next one begins.

- You don't have to write on every page. Fill in only those pages that are relevant or meaningful to you.

- Start anywhere you want. You can go straight through from the first to last prompt or skip around.

Who? And when?

- You can enjoy filling in this book whether you were married recently or many years ago.

- If you are newly married, fill it out as you go along, like a journal.

- If you are well along in your relationship, you will be able to fill out most of it now, like an autobiography.

- You can fill it out alone for your own enjoyment,

- Or you can fill it out together as a way to remember, share, and record your love story.

What do we do with this book after it is filled out?

- You can keep the completed journal private for your own pleasure,

- Or give it as a special gift to your partner. You can present it as an expression of your love any time, or on an anniversary, birthday or Valentine's Day.

- Share it with children, grandchildren and others. Generations to come will treasure this record of your marriage.

- Read it cover to cover; reflect and rejoice in the wonder of your love story.

Introduction

Kate's story

I was raised by storytellers. Gathered around the dinner table, we told true stories and imaginative tall tales. One story that captivated me as a young girl was the story my parents told of how they met. What fascinated me was the discovery that they hadn't always been middle-aged parents as I knew them then; that what I was seeing at that moment was just the middle of a love story. I still love to hear couples tell how they met, how they fell in love, and what joys and surprises they've found along the way.

I was born near Boston, Massachusetts, in 1959. I never thought I would fall in love with a boy from Texas, until I met David. I've learned a lot about myself and the world through my dance with David, and I don't ever plan to take off my dancing shoes. One of the many gifts he has given me has been to show me a truly generous soul. I am in awe of someone who can give away the very last brownie, and feel good about it.

David's story

I was born in Dallas, Texas, in 1956 and all my relatives still live in Texas and Oklahoma. As a Methodist minister's son, I was always on the road growing up. I lived in Chicago, Kansas, South Carolina, Germany, Malaysia, California, and Colorado before meeting Kate during the fall of 1981 in New York City, where we had both just started working for the same company. I still remember when I first saw Kate as we rode up in the packed elevator. I thought, "Wow, who is the beautiful, tall

woman standing in the corner? Hope she gets off at my floor."
She did.

Several years ago I cowrote a book with my grandfather shortly before he died: *The Book of Myself*, which helps people write their own do-it-yourself autobiographies. Hyperion and Disney Publishing believed in the power of family storytelling and published this book in 1997. In the same spirit, Kate and I wrote this book to help people capture the love relationship. So, *The Book of Us* was born.

After we wrote this book, we "road tested" it by filling it out ourselves. Since we are in our middle years, we were able to fill out most of it. We laughed and cried as we remembered some of the precious and painful moments along the way. We hope our children, Emily and Ben, will enjoy reading about the love that inspired their birth and nurturing. As we approach our fifteenth wedding anniversary, we are still deeply in love and look forward to creating many more love stories together. "Later Years," here we come!

In love relationships there are three parts: me, you and us. All three deserve a chance to have their story recorded. All three are compelling, both to the main characters and to the generations that follow. This journal lets you tell the story of your "us."

Getting to Know You

$\mathcal{B}$efore I met you, my love life was ...

_____

_____

_____

_____

_____

_____

_____

_____

_____

_____

_____

_____

_____

If this had not happened, we never would have met....

_____

_____

_____

_____

_____

_____

_____

_____

_____

_____

_____

$\mathcal{T}$his is how I remember the first time we met....

_____

_____

_____

_____

_____

_____

_____

_____

_____

_____

_____

_____

_____

_____

*M*y very first impression of you and what initially attracted me to you was . . .

_____

_____

_____

_____

_____

_____

_____

_____

_____

_____

_____

_____

_____

The Book of Us

$\mathcal{I}$ knew I wanted to see more of you when . . .

_____

_____

_____

_____

_____

_____

_____

_____

_____

_____

_____

_____

$\mathcal{T}$his is how our first date was arranged....

_____

_____

_____

_____

_____

_____

_____

_____

_____

_____

_____

_____

On our first date we ...

_____

_____

_____

_____

_____

_____

_____

_____

_____

_____

_____

_____

_____

Some things we did on our early dates were ...

_____

_____

_____

_____

_____

_____

_____

_____

_____

_____

_____

_____

_____

We saw these movies, performances and events
together....

_____

_____

_____

_____

_____

_____

_____

_____

_____

_____

_____

_____

_____

_____

As I saw more of you, what really made me fall in love was . . .

_____

_____

_____

_____

_____

_____

_____

_____

_____

_____

_____

_____

$\mathcal{J}$ knew that you just might be "the one" when ...

_____

_____

_____

_____

_____

_____

_____

_____

_____

_____

_____

_____

_____

$\mathcal{A}$n obstacle in the path of our romance early on was . . .

_____

_____

_____

_____

_____

_____

_____

_____

_____

_____

_____

Rivals for your love or mine were...

$\mathcal{A}$ special intimate moment or time was when . . .

_____

_____

_____

_____

_____

_____

_____

_____

_____

_____

_____

_____

*O*ur families were different and similar in these ways. . . .

The first time I met your family . . .

_____

_____

_____

_____

_____

_____

_____

_____

_____

_____

_____

_____

_____

The first time you met my family ...

_____

_____

_____

_____

_____

_____

_____

_____

_____

_____

_____

_____

_____

$\mathcal{H}$ere's what family and friends had to say about us as we became a couple....

_____

_____

_____

_____

_____

_____

_____

_____

_____

_____

_____

_____

_____

_____

$\mathcal{T}$he following people encouraged our romance. . . .

_____

_____

_____

_____

_____

_____

_____

_____

_____

_____

_____

_____

_____

_____

When we were apart, we stayed in touch by . . .

_____

_____

_____

_____

_____

_____

_____

_____

_____

_____

_____

_____

_____

$\mathcal{S}$ome of the most popular songs during this period of our relationship were . . .

_____

_____

_____

_____

_____

_____

_____

_____

_____

_____

_____

_____

$\mathcal{S}$ports played this role in our romance. . . .

_____

_____

_____

_____

_____

_____

_____

_____

_____

_____

_____

_____

_____

$\mathcal{T}$hese things symbolized our growing love (special song, place, poem, etc.)....

_____

_____

_____

_____

_____

_____

_____

_____

_____

_____

_____

_____

_____

_____

World and community events that occurred during this time in our relationship were . . .

_____

_____

_____

_____

_____

_____

_____

_____

_____

_____

_____

_____

We shared this vision for the future. . . .

_____

_____

_____

_____

_____

_____

_____

_____

_____

_____

_____

_____

_____

We had these differences to work out. . . .

_____

_____

_____

_____

_____

_____

_____

_____

_____

_____

_____

_____

S pecial premarriage milestones I remember are (first meeting, first date, first kiss, etc.) . . .

_____

_____

_____

_____

_____

_____

_____

_____

_____

_____

_____

_____

_____

*S*ome of the things we both believed in were . . .

_____

_____

_____

_____

_____

_____

_____

_____

_____

_____

_____

_____

_____

Our romance almost broke up when . . .

_____

_____

_____

_____

_____

_____

_____

_____

_____

_____

_____

_____

_____

$\mathcal{I}$ remember this fight (or disagreement) and how we resolved it. . . .

_____

_____

_____

_____

_____

_____

_____

_____

_____

_____

_____

_____

*O*ne of the most beautiful things about you was . . .

_____

_____

_____

_____

_____

_____

_____

_____

_____

_____

_____

_____

If I was scared about getting serious with you it was because . . .

_____

_____

_____

_____

_____

_____

_____

_____

_____

_____

_____

_____

*S*omething else I want to say about this time in our relationship is . . .

_____

_____

_____

_____

_____

_____

_____

_____

_____

_____

_____

_____

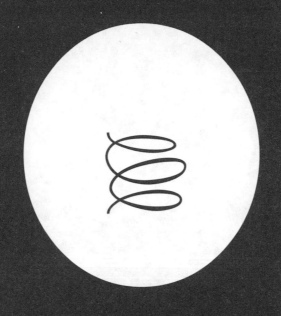

Tying the Knot

$\mathcal{I}$ talked with the following people about marrying you before making a decision. Their advice was . . .

_____

_____

_____

_____

_____

_____

_____

_____

_____

_____

_____

_____

_____

When you proposed to me (or I proposed to you)...

_____

_____

_____

_____

_____

_____

_____

_____

_____

_____

_____

_____

_____

$\mathcal{T}$his is how we approached our parents with our decision. . . .

_____

_____

_____

_____

_____

_____

_____

_____

_____

_____

_____

_____

_____

*T*hese are some of the reactions we got when announcing our engagement (and wedding date)....

_____

_____

_____

_____

_____

_____

_____

_____

_____

_____

_____

_____

We decided to do these important things before marrying....

_____

_____

_____

_____

_____

_____

_____

_____

_____

_____

_____

_____

$\mathcal{T}$his is how and why we chose the engagement and wedding rings we did. . . .

_____

_____

_____

_____

_____

_____

_____

_____

_____

_____

_____

_____

_____

$\mathcal{T}$his is how we decided to handle changing or not changing names....

_____

_____

_____

_____

_____

_____

_____

_____

_____

_____

_____

_____

When thinking about the kind of wedding we wanted, we agreed and disagreed about these things....

_____

_____

_____

_____

_____

_____

_____

_____

_____

_____

_____

_____

*O*ur families influenced the kind of wedding
we planned in these ways. . . .

_____

_____

_____

_____

_____

_____

_____

_____

_____

_____

_____

_____

_____

$\mathcal{T}$he main wedding planners, and how they helped, included...

_____

_____

_____

_____

_____

_____

_____

_____

_____

_____

_____

_____

_____

$\mathcal{T}$his is what the wedding dress looked like and why it was picked. . . .

_____

_____

_____

_____

_____

_____

_____

_____

_____

_____

_____

_____

_____

*T*he wedding officiator (clergy, rabbi or other) helped us think these things through. . . .

_____

_____

_____

_____

_____

_____

_____

_____

_____

_____

_____

_____

_____

A funny thing that happened during the planning of the wedding or the wedding itself was...

_____

_____

_____

_____

_____

_____

_____

_____

_____

_____

_____

_____

_____

*T*he cast of wedding party members, and why they were chosen, included ...

_____

_____

_____

_____

_____

_____

_____

_____

_____

_____

_____

_____

_____

_____

$\mathcal{T}$he wedding location, and why it was chosen, was ...

_____

_____

_____

_____

_____

_____

_____

_____

_____

_____

_____

_____

_____

_____

The pre-wedding parties (bachelor, bride, other) went like this....

_____

_____

_____

_____

_____

_____

_____

_____

_____

_____

_____

_____

_____

$\mathcal{T}$hese were some last-minute glitches. . . .

_____

_____

_____

_____

_____

_____

_____

_____

_____

_____

_____

_____

_____

$\mathcal{I}$ remember this about getting ready for the big moment. . . .

_____

_____

_____

_____

_____

_____

_____

_____

_____

_____

_____

_____

_____

*S*pecial conversations, with each other or with others, before the ceremony were . . .

_____

_____

_____

_____

_____

_____

_____

_____

_____

_____

_____

_____

_____

$\mathcal{S}$ pecial guests at the wedding and some people we wished could have been there included . . .

_____

_____

_____

_____

_____

_____

_____

_____

_____

_____

_____

_____

_____

The ceremony itself included ...

_____

_____

_____

_____

_____

_____

_____

_____

_____

_____

_____

_____

_____

$\mathcal{T}$o me, the marriage vows meant this. . . .

_____

_____

_____

_____

_____

_____

_____

_____

_____

_____

_____

_____

$\mathcal{A}$fter the wedding we all celebrated in this way. . . .

_____

_____

_____

_____

_____

_____

_____

_____

_____

_____

_____

_____

_____

_____

*S*ome of the best moments at the reception
celebration were...

_____

_____

_____

_____

_____

_____

_____

_____

_____

_____

_____

_____

_____

*T*he most special part of the whole day was . . .

_____

_____

_____

_____

_____

_____

_____

_____

_____

_____

_____

_____

_____

_____

_____

We spent our wedding night . . .

_____

_____

_____

_____

_____

_____

_____

_____

_____

_____

_____

_____

_____

*T*his is where we went for our honeymoon and what we did....

_____

_____

_____

_____

_____

_____

_____

_____

_____

_____

_____

_____

What I loved about our honeymoon was...

We discovered these things about each other on our honeymoon....

_____

_____

_____

_____

_____

_____

_____

_____

_____

_____

_____

_____

$\mathcal{S}$omething else I want to say about this time in our relationship is . . .

_____

_____

_____

_____

_____

_____

_____

_____

_____

_____

_____

_____

Starting Out Together

When we were starting out, this is the future we hoped for. . . .

_____

_____

_____

_____

_____

_____

_____

_____

_____

_____

_____

_____

The first place(s) we lived as a married couple was (were)...

_____

_____

_____

_____

_____

_____

_____

_____

_____

_____

_____

_____

We bought our first home...

_____

_____

_____

_____

_____

_____

_____

_____

_____

_____

_____

_____

_____

*C*ombining our belongings and deciding what to buy new went like this. . . .

_____

_____

_____

_____

_____

_____

_____

_____

_____

_____

_____

_____

$\mathcal{T}$his is how our finances were set up early on. . . .

_____

_____

_____

_____

_____

_____

_____

_____

_____

_____

_____

_____

_____

This challenged our relationship....

*T*hese were couples or single friends we enjoyed spending time with and what we did. . . .

_____

_____

_____

_____

_____

_____

_____

_____

_____

_____

_____

_____

_____

_____

*L*iving together taught us these new things about each other (and our habits)....

_____

_____

_____

_____

_____

_____

_____

_____

_____

_____

_____

_____

We shared some romantic moments on Valentine's Days....

_____

_____

_____

_____

_____

_____

_____

_____

_____

_____

_____

_____

$\mathcal{I}$ admired and was inspired by the following couple(s) (famous or otherwise)....

_____

_____

_____

_____

_____

_____

_____

_____

_____

_____

_____

_____

_____

We started talking about having children . . .

_____

_____

_____

_____

_____

_____

_____

_____

_____

_____

_____

_____

_____

If we had children, the birth of our first child (and others) was amazing....

_____

_____

_____

_____

_____

_____

_____

_____

_____

_____

_____

_____

_____

*H*aving children changed our relationship in these ways during this period....

_____

_____

_____

_____

_____

_____

_____

_____

_____

_____

_____

_____

_____

$\mathcal{D}$uring the first year of our relationship, it changed in this way. . . .

_____

_____

_____

_____

_____

_____

_____

_____

_____

_____

_____

_____

_____

$\mathcal{T}$his was a great trip we took together. . . .

_____

_____

_____

_____

_____

_____

_____

_____

_____

_____

_____

_____

_____

Our _____ anniversary was particularly memorable because . . .

_____

_____

_____

_____

_____

_____

_____

_____

_____

_____

_____

_____

_____

$\mathcal{D}$ifferences in our backgrounds and personalities sometimes showed up in these ways....

_____

_____

_____

_____

_____

_____

_____

_____

_____

_____

_____

_____

_____

_____

$\mathcal{T}$hese were some disagreements and how we resolved them....

_____

_____

_____

_____

_____

_____

_____

_____

_____

_____

_____

These are some ways we took care of each other....

_____

_____

_____

_____

_____

_____

_____

_____

_____

_____

_____

_____

_____

_____

$\mathcal{I}$ really felt close to you when . . .

I missed you when ...

We used these special nicknames with each other....

_____

_____

_____

_____

_____

_____

_____

_____

_____

_____

_____

_____

$\mathcal{J}$ know it really bothered you when I...

_____

_____

_____

_____

_____

_____

_____

_____

_____

_____

_____

_____

_____

_____

$\mathcal{J}$t really bothered me when you ...

This is how a typical week went....

_____

_____

_____

_____

_____

_____

_____

_____

_____

_____

_____

_____

$\mathcal{T}$his is how we divided the household chores. . . .

_____

_____

_____

_____

_____

_____

_____

_____

_____

_____

_____

_____

$\mathcal{Y}$ou supported me in my work in this way....

_____

_____

_____

_____

_____

_____

_____

_____

_____

_____

_____

_____

_____

_____

$\mathcal{I}$ tried to support you in your work in this way. . . .

_____

_____

_____

_____

_____

_____

_____

_____

_____

_____

_____

_____

$\mathcal{T}$hese are some traditions we established for holidays....

_____

_____

_____

_____

_____

_____

_____

_____

_____

_____

_____

_____

_____

We had fun doing these things. . . .

_____

_____

_____

_____

_____

_____

_____

_____

_____

_____

_____

_____

Music we listened to and shows we enjoyed included...

_____

_____

_____

_____

_____

_____

_____

_____

_____

_____

_____

_____

_____

These things really made us laugh....

_____

_____

_____

_____

_____

_____

_____

_____

_____

_____

_____

_____

These outside world events affected us. . . .

_____

_____

_____

_____

_____

_____

_____

_____

_____

_____

_____

_____

_____

_____

_____

_____

_____

_____

_____

_____

_____

_____

_____

_____

_____

The Middle Years

*J*f we had children, this is how they affected our
relationship during this time....

_____

_____

_____

_____

_____

_____

_____

_____

_____

_____

_____

_____

_____

$\mathcal{T}$his was particularly joyful for us as parents ...

_____

_____

_____

_____

_____

_____

_____

_____

_____

_____

_____

_____

_____

_____

J appreciated this about the way you parented our children....

_____

_____

_____

_____

_____

_____

_____

_____

_____

_____

_____

_____

_____

$\mathcal{T}$his was especially hard for us as parents...

_____

_____

_____

_____

_____

_____

_____

_____

_____

_____

_____

_____

_____

_____

We agreed and disagreed about politics and community affairs in this way....

_____

_____

_____

_____

_____

_____

_____

_____

_____

_____

_____

_____

_____

Our outside responsibilities (work, volunteer activities, other) affected each other in this way. . . .

_____

_____

_____

_____

_____

_____

_____

_____

_____

_____

_____

_____

_____

*W*e supported each other in our jobs by . . .

We worked to balance the needs of career and family by . . .

_____

_____

_____

_____

_____

_____

_____

_____

_____

_____

_____

_____

I was proud to be your spouse when ...

_____

_____

_____

_____

_____

_____

_____

_____

_____

_____

_____

_____

_____

_____

A memorable hobby or project we worked on together was ...

_____

_____

_____

_____

_____

_____

_____

_____

_____

_____

_____

_____

_____

_____

A house project to remember was ...

_____

_____

_____

_____

_____

_____

_____

_____

_____

_____

_____

_____

Our most difficult and our best financial periods were...

_____

_____

_____

_____

_____

_____

_____

_____

_____

_____

_____

_____

*W*hen we were able to put other duties aside,
we liked to relax together by . . .

_____

_____

_____

_____

_____

_____

_____

_____

_____

_____

_____

_____

*W*e spent a lot of time with these people, and this is what we did with them. . . .

_____

_____

_____

_____

_____

_____

_____

_____

_____

_____

_____

$\mathcal{T}$his was a memorable party we gave or attended....

_____

_____

_____

_____

_____

_____

_____

_____

_____

_____

_____

_____

_____

*T*hese were a few of the everyday routines we had....

_____

_____

_____

_____

_____

_____

_____

_____

_____

_____

_____

We spent our weekends ...

*O*ur relationship evolved over the years in this way....

One of my favorite vacations we took together was . . .

_____

_____

_____

_____

_____

_____

_____

_____

_____

_____

_____

_____

We celebrated this special anniversary by . . .

_____

_____

_____

_____

_____

_____

_____

_____

_____

_____

_____

_____

_____

_____

A very sad time for us was when . . .

_____

_____

_____

_____

_____

_____

_____

_____

_____

_____

_____

_____

_____

J appreciated your family when they ...

_____

_____

_____

_____

_____

_____

_____

_____

_____

_____

_____

_____

_____

_____

$y$ou taught me how to . . .

_____

_____

_____

_____

_____

_____

_____

_____

_____

_____

_____

_____

$\mathcal{S}$ome ways we showed affection for each other included...

_____

_____

_____

_____

_____

_____

_____

_____

_____

_____

_____

_____

We went through this crisis and came out stronger....

_____

_____

_____

_____

_____

_____

_____

_____

_____

_____

_____

_____

_____

$\mathcal{J}$ remember this funny story. . . .

_____

_____

_____

_____

_____

_____

_____

_____

_____

_____

_____

_____

_____

_____

$\mathcal{I}$ loved hearing you tell these stories....

_____

_____

_____

_____

_____

_____

_____

_____

_____

_____

_____

_____

_____

_____

$\mathcal{S}$omething else I want to say about this time in our relationship is . . .

_____

_____

_____

_____

_____

_____

_____

_____

_____

_____

_____

_____

The Later Years

Our _____ anniversary celebration was an event to remember. . . .

_____

_____

_____

_____

_____

_____

_____

_____

_____

_____

_____

_____

We made some changes to our living situation in these years (new home, location, job, help, etc.)....

_____

_____

_____

_____

_____

_____

_____

_____

_____

_____

_____

Exploring new directions brought new adventures for us as a couple (vocation, religion, interests, other)....

_____

_____

_____

_____

_____

_____

_____

_____

_____

_____

_____

_____

When our children became adults, it changed
our lives as a couple by . . .

_____

_____

_____

_____

_____

_____

_____

_____

_____

_____

_____

_____

_____

$\mathcal{A}$fter we retired, we had more time to . . .

_____

_____

_____

_____

_____

_____

_____

_____

_____

_____

_____

_____

_____

_____

We traveled to these places. . . .

_____

_____

_____

_____

_____

_____

_____

_____

_____

_____

_____

_____

_____

If we became grandparents, this is what we did with our grandchildren....

_____

_____

_____

_____

_____

_____

_____

_____

_____

_____

_____

_____

_____

$\mathcal{A}$fter all these years, I learned this new aspect about you. . . .

_____

_____

_____

_____

_____

_____

_____

_____

_____

_____

_____

_____

_____

$\mathcal{S}$ome hobbies we enjoyed together and some apart....

_____

_____

_____

_____

_____

_____

_____

_____

_____

_____

_____

The hard part for our relationship after retirement was...

_____

_____

_____

_____

_____

_____

_____

_____

_____

_____

_____

_____

_____

I am thankful for your help with ...

_____

_____

_____

_____

_____

_____

_____

_____

_____

_____

_____

_____

_____

_____

Of all the many gifts you've given me, the most precious one is . . .

_____

_____

_____

_____

_____

_____

_____

_____

_____

_____

_____

_____

I appreciate your teaching me these things. . . .

_____

_____

_____

_____

_____

_____

_____

_____

_____

_____

_____

_____

Without your help, I never could have (or would have)...

_____

_____

_____

_____

_____

_____

_____

_____

_____

_____

_____

_____

_____

We approached a major health problem in this manner. . . .

_____

_____

_____

_____

_____

_____

_____

_____

_____

_____

_____

_____

_____

_____

As our bodies grew older, this is how it affected our relationship (hearing loss, etc.)....

_____

_____

_____

_____

_____

_____

_____

_____

_____

_____

_____

We mourned the loss of this dear person (or people) together. . . .

_____

_____

_____

_____

_____

_____

_____

_____

_____

_____

_____

_____

_____

$\mathcal{A}$ lesson or two about marriage I'd like to share with the next generation is ...

_____

_____

_____

_____

_____

_____

_____

_____

_____

_____

_____

_____

One of the reasons I think we lasted so long as a couple is that . . .

_____

_____

_____

_____

_____

_____

_____

_____

_____

_____

_____

_____

_____

_____

_____

_____

_____

_____

_____

_____

_____

_____

_____

_____

_____

$\mathcal{J}$ have enjoyed this specialty of yours (recipe, craft, talent, etc.)....

_____

_____

_____

_____

_____

_____

_____

_____

_____

_____

_____

_____

*T*his is a story I love to tell about us (from any time period)....

_____

_____

_____

_____

_____

_____

_____

_____

_____

_____

_____

_____

_____

*T*hese are the qualities you have that I love most....

_____

_____

_____

_____

_____

_____

_____

_____

_____

_____

_____

_____

_____

$\mathcal{S}$omething else I want to say about this time in our relationship is ...

_____

_____

_____

_____

_____

_____

_____

_____

_____

_____

_____

_____

_____

_____

Our own special title of *The Book of Us* could be . . .

_____

_____

_____

_____

_____

_____

_____

_____

_____

_____

_____

_____

About the Authors

During their seventeen years of courtship and marriage, Kate and David Marshall have lived in New York City, Mexico City, Atlanta, Cambridge, Mass., Munich and the San Francisco Bay area. Their children, Emily and Ben, are the other loves in their lives.

Kate manages the marketing program for a publishing company. She also counsels callers in crisis on a hotline and coordinates parent education for local schools. Kate and David are the co-authors of *The Book of My Pet*.

David is a marketing executive in a leading adult education software firm and is the co-author of *The Book of Myself*.

If you have any thoughts about the book, please send them to:

Kate and David Marshall
PO Box 6846
Moraga, CA 94570-6846

Or send us an email message: dpmars@ix.netcom.com